Outlandish Blues

Also by Honorée Fanonne Jeffers:

The Gospel of Barbecue, 2000

Outlandish Blues

Honorée Fanonne Jeffers

Wesleyan University Press

MIDDLETOWN, CONNECTICUT

Published by Wesleyan University Press, Middletown, CT 06459
© 2003 by Honorée Fanonne Jeffers
All rights reserved
Printed in the United States of America
5 4 3 2 1

CIP data appear at the back of the book

Grateful acknowledgment is given to the publications where these poems first appeared,
some in earlier form with different titles:

Black Warrior Review: "The Book of Alabama: Chapter Coltrane"
BMa: The Sonia Sanchez Review: "Now with the Morning"
Brilliant Corners: A Journal of Jazz and Literature: "Worn Blues Refrain"
Callaloo: "Confederate Pride Day at Bama (Tuscaloosa, 1994)," "The Wife of Lot Before
    the Fire," "The Wife of Lot Has a Premonition of Her Death," "The Wife of Lot Wit-
    nesses Her Husband Offering Their Two Daughters to Sodom's Crowd," and "The
    Wife of Lot After the Fire"
The Kenyon Review—New Series, Summer/Fall 2002, Vol. XXIV, No. ¾: "Hagar to Sarai"
The Massachusetts Review: "Don't Know What Love Is," "Five Note Range of Sorrow," and
    "Think of James Brown Pleading"
Ploughshares: "Aretha at Fame Studios"
Prairie Schooner: "Sarai Gives Hagar the Egyptian to Abram," "Hagar's Night With Abram,"
    "Sarai Waits for the Birth of Hagar's Son," "Sarah Gives Birth to Isaac," "Sarah Con-
    fronts Abraham Over Hagar," and "Hagar in the Wilderness"

For *Mama*

and

for *Mr. Langston Hughes,*

poet laureate of the blues

CONTENTS

III.

ACKNOWLEDGMENTS

Gratitude first and always to the Creator, from Whom all words and life descend, and to the ancestors for watching over.

To my family: Trellie James Jeffers, Valjeanne Jeffers Thompson, Sidonie Jeffers, Toussaint Thompson, Gabrielle Thompson, and Mikail Thompson.

Many thanks to Cornelius Eady, Cynthia Hogue, Afaa Michael Weaver, Sarah Micklem, Carolyn Micklem, Natasha Trethewey, Lori Amy, Heidi Durrow, James Richardson, Jr., Andrea Franckowiak, Grace Paley, Jerry Ward, Jr., Hank Lazer, Myron Tuman, Herman Beavers, Maggie Anderson, Fred Hord, and Terry Duffy.

I

Fast Skirt Blues

for V.

You Mama's son. You
sister's brother. You
baby's Daddy. You
woman's husband. You,

take me someplace.
Help me burn off a midnight crazy.
The tune in this head as hard

to hold as smoke in my clothes.
Tell me what ails me, baby.
I ain't got no shame—that's
what I say to myself.

I want to teach you the pigmeat
story this evening. I'm an angel
stabbed by the point I dance on.

I need the sanctified blues.
I need the hallelujah nasty.
Take me there.
I don't care where we go.

Out past County Line Road
and a dark field shout.
On a cracked backseat.

On my big brass bed.
I don't care.
I'll sing you the gap-legged
words the last man heard,

explain how I got born
with this sorry caul on my face.
You know a bad girl's gone

pay for her sugar one day:
I know it,
God knows it.
Now, the Devil do, too.

Muse, a Lady Cautioning

for Billie Holiday

There's fairness in changing blood for septet's
guardian rhythm, the horn blossoming
into cadenza. No good pimp's scowl, his
baby's voice ruined sweet for the duration.

Yes, these predictable fifths. O, the blues
is all about slinging those low tales out
the back door (sing: child pried open on that
stained floor). O, Billie hollers way down dirt

roads (sing: woman on the verge of needled
logic). She's aware—yeah, I'm going to
kiss some man's sugared fist tonight. O, this
tableau's muse, a Lady cautioning me:

Just tough this thing out, girl. Sweat through the jones.
Don't ask for nothing. Spit your last damned note.

The Battered Blues (Four Movements)

1. Jones for My Blues

My man the kind of man don't like a soul
hanging 'round his house when he won't at home
I should have known not to answer the door
My man the kind of man don't trust a soul
So when he put me on his highest shelf
I just kept my lonely to myself

I've been downhearted ever since the day we met

He hit me most times for being quiet
He hit me once or twice for keeping still
He made my face red clay between his hands
and shaped me over again in his bed
Every morning and I was leaving
Then nighttime fell and he was on his knees
He cried and screamed that he would surely die
but I was gone join him in the boneyard

Misery on my porch and sadness on my steps
I've been downhearted ever since the day we met

I must admit I played the fool long
after I knew the story of this man
and kept on till the last day I was through
You know he won't never gone let me stand
I washed off his dust and his sorry pain
bought me a switchblade shouting out his name

It was clear this man had a jones for my blues
The tune as far from love as one bullet can get
I've been downhearted ever since the day we met

2. Turning the Other Cheek

My shrink says I need to get out
of my man's house while I still
can but I can't pay her if I leave him.

My preacher says I need to pray
and learn to be like Jesus, turn
my cheek until I hear the word of God.

My mother says I need to be like her,
a good woman who loved the sound
of my father's dinner bell like one of Pavlov's dogs.

My man says I can't be happy,
no I won't be happy
until I make him happy, too.

I think about the sound of my blues
and need without end, the nights when
the dark takes the shape of my master's voice.

3. Preparing the Escape

When you're finally ready to leave
When you've packed all your bags
When you say you've had enough
of your man's flying fists and you don't care
if you throw everything behind you
That's when he seems to be all places at the same time
You better check under the beds and open the doors
You better look in your rear view mirror
before you drive into the street
He could be following you
and that's the last thing you need
And don't you get out of your car
And don't you try to reason with him
And don't you let him scare you
And don't you let him charm you
And don't you feel sorry for him
And don't you listen to him howl
his blues and believe he will wrap
up the whole world for you
You'll be crying with that man and out
of nowhere he'll kill your children first
and then he'll kill you
and maybe he'll kill himself
but not before he's finished singing

4. At the Shelter

They tell me the deal. If I threaten
to harm my man, talk about a real
plan to take him out for good,
they'll call the cops right away so they
at least can save somebody.—This is
regulation and I better remember that.

I'm going to kill him
I'm going to stab him in his sleep
I'm going to send him back to God
and pray my soul to keep

They say they won't wait for disaster
at three o'clock in the morning but then
they never ask why I didn't leave him.
Before I have to keep in a water glass
the only teeth he didn't knock out.
They won't mock a woman running
away in the night, dragging the children
who jump and cry at shadows.

You know I might kill him
I might stab him in his sleep
I might send him back to God
and pray my soul to keep

They know sooner or later the truth comes
down heavy on every one of us,
the nature of love digging in its nails.
I know they won't turn me in, not to the cops,
not to my man. They won't listen to my blues
a moment too soon, just say nothing
and wait until my bruises fade.

You know he's going to kill me
He's going to stab me in my sleep
He's going to send me back to God
and pray his soul to keep

Don't Know What Love Is

My mother can't recall the exact
infamous year but Mama does know
that she and her friends were teenagers
when they sneaked out to an official joint
in the middle of the woods to listen
to Dinah Washington sing their favorite
love song. They wanted to dance together
so close they'd be standing behind
each other but Mama says, *Dinah showed*
up late and acted ugly and on top of
that she didn't want to sing the song.
This is supposed to be the story of Mama's
blues and how she threw good money
after bad but this is South Georgia
and Dinah's standing in high heels on a Jim
Crow stage two feet off the ground.
She's sniffing the perfume of homemade
cigarettes, chitlin plates, hair grease one
grade above Vaseline, and the premature
funk wafting up from the rowdy kids
with no home training. Can't even pee
straight much less recognize a silver lamé
dress. All they know to do is demand
one song because they risked a certain
butt whipping to be in this joint, in these woods.
Dinah won't sing it, though.
She just won't sing the song.
I'm an evil gal, she hollers out instead.
Don't you bother with me!

Worn Blues Refrain

My father danced on Saturday mornings,
turned his fat professor's legs the wrong way.
No rhythm self, tripping over Mama's corns,
his jitterbug like a worn blues refrain.
Then the afternoons, he sat himself down
to the piano, knee pants memories
of Louis and his trumpet come to town.
Louis didn't crack a smile. *Don't believe?*
Want to dispute it? Dad didn't think so
and commenced with Jelly Roll religion.
Those porcelain hours, demons stopped poking
my father. From someplace close he found love.
He got some rhythm when he played the blues,
hollered and touched us all without bruising.

Pantoum for a Black Man on a Greyhound Bus

I just met him and he looks out the window, cries,
tells me he spent fifteen years behind prison walls.
What I can say to him is a weak *welcome home*.
I can't find vocabulary to resolve absence.

He left fifteen years behind prison walls.
Anne Sexton used to call her asylum a jail.
I wish there were vocabulary to resolve absence,
to name the fight past newborn insanity.

Anne Sexton used to call her asylum a jail.
I don't want to know how this brother earned his cell.
He's fighting his way past newborn insanity,
weeping for his mother and her useless songs.

I don't want to know what earned him a cell.
My real brother's mother died on her kitchen floor.
What of that night? What of her useless songs?
Did my brother hear the prayers breaking in her hands?

I think of my stepmother murdered on her floor:
at twenty-nine, my brother became his father's son.
What of those prayers breaking in Camille's hands?
For whose sake should my brother be forgiven?

At twenty-nine, my brother became his father's son,
the trail of blood beginning at the sire's gate.
For whose sake should my brother be forgiven?
Am I a woman or am I my brother's keeper?

My brothers spill blood at their sisters' gates
while we watch our doors with uneasy eyes.
Are we supposed to be our brothers' keepers
when those children return as sullen men?

And here I watch my door with uneasy eyes,
hoping I can welcome my brother home:
a child who returns as a grown man,
who looks out the window and cries to himself.

Think of James Brown Pleading

for Michael Datcher

As if on cue, the women
in the room start screaming,
snagged on your words
as you sing of sugar distilled.
You're reading a love poem
and have to stop for a few moments
in the middle, your voice breaking,
and I wonder if a spirit can be
reincarnated before it dies.
I think of James Brown pleading
to a closing door. So pretty
in his do-rag tied on straight
through the day and into the night
and right now, you are prettier
than James. The brothers in the room
wink and nod at your raw weeping
but what man trusts another at his
most dangerous? This is the truth
I need: your crying and holding
fast to one woman at the same time.
What else is left if I can ignore your
tears or James, shoulders
draped with female screams
and royal purple, begging with all
the sweat he was capable of?

II

Sarai Gives Hagar the Egyptian to Abram

> Now Sarai Abram's wife bare him no children: and she had
> an handmaid, an Egyptian, whose name was Hagar.
>
> GEN. 16:1

I need a child so please make me one dear
sacrifice. Hold the sheep by his cleaved hooves,
slit the throat and watch the blood rain down loud.
Cut a foreskin, pray there is God in the deed.
I am a seed dried from the inside out.
I am a hull cracked open in the sand.
Waiting for Someone's kiss on His way up
yonder, waiting for knowing in my bones.
Don't know why my house keeps getting passed by.
Don't know why my Lord won't touch me holy.
Laugh out loud at visions born every night,
cry each day at my arms waking empty.
Give me something. Give me a sacrifice.
Why won't just one angel come on by here?

Hagar's Night with Abram

Only God knows how I feel
this night when I'm locked
together with the man.
God of Eve,
God of daughters with no names,
God of mother's sons driven away,
God of handmaids passed around
like stew in a bowl,
God knows I wish I could be
ready and beloved.
One name spoken from holy lips,
a splinter of heaven and a *Yes my Lord yes.*
I wish I could give gratitude right now,
this night, before I become lowered
eyes and covered head again,
borrowed linen and wine and skin.

Sarai Waits for the Birth of Hagar's Son

When you gone show
that child kicking
through your skin

Need to sing praises
of a sucking thumb
Need to wrap your

belly in new linen
When will you
lie down in my bed

Somebody's coming
Sparrow's eye watching
a man filling your heart

Guide my feet
near your milky river
Somebody's coming

Somebody's coming
speaking in tongues
to marks on your waist

Hagar to Sarai

Don't give me nothing in
exchange for a beating
in my belly, sore nipples
way after the sucking is gone.
Don't thank me for my body,
a fine drinking skin
turned inside out for you.
Don't thank me for the back
that don't break from Abram's weight.
I know what you need—a baby's
wail in the morning,
smile on your man's face,
his loins full of much obliged.
I know what you need;
don't give me your grief
to help this thing along.
I know how emptiness feels.
Woman, I know how
to make my own tears.

Sarah Overhears the Three Angels Telling Abraham God Will Destroy Sodom

I'm trying to remember
I been with you since
dirt touched water

Since the morning burned
our faces lovely
there is a life we had
carved into one skin

The Word long ago
a much happy getting
glad at day clean

Man with lined grace
will we die together
Can we find blessings
with these changed names

Hard days fire days
my praises your shouts
are swallowed quiet

Sometimes I can't remember
to send up a mended song
Forget to bend my
knees and pray for rain

The Wife of Lot Before the Fire

First time I lay with him
music came from my mouth
I ain't never heard
such strong music

You the one gone save me
You the one gone take me
away from here

Lately a humming
coming from the other
corners of this house
The whispering

His walking in the night hours
His blood on the backs
of our daughters' skirts

Baby please
You the one gone save me
You the one supposed
to take me away from here

Lately a humming
coming from the other
corners of this house

First time I lay with him
who knew I could
reach those notes
Now I done forgot his tune

The man said a thief
done plucked my tongue
right from my singing throat

The Wife of Lot Has a Premonition
of Her Death

If I wanted to speak, I could make Him see
there was no fairness in these Cain and Abel games.
First you love one, then the other.
Now a man will be saved, now a woman will die.
Both sides lose when you gamble like that.
Two causes for tears called a name together.

Soon one morning
Death come creeping in my room

Didn't I learn by myself to pray?
Didn't I sing only one name?
Didn't I give the first offerings of my tongue?
Didn't I open my soul to my old man's seed?
Day each one of these girls was born,
didn't I slip my fingers under her crown,
cup the new head resting against my palm?
Can't any of that buy me one thing?

Soon one morning
Death come creeping in my room

Maybe I'm not just a plain-formed woman.
Maybe I'm Eve becoming sin.
Maybe I've learned what is harder than a curse.
I can make my own earth
and oceans and little beasts.
Maybe this man's God is afraid of me.

Soon one morning
Death come creeping in my room
O my Lord   O my Lord
What shall I do

The Wife of Lot Witnesses Her Husband Offering Their Two Daughters to Sodom's Crowd

> There came two angels to Sodom at even: and Lot sat at the gate of
> Sodom . . . and he said Behold now, my lords, turn in, I pray you, into
> your servant's house . . . But before they lay down, the men of the city,
> compassed the house round. . .
>
> GEN. 19:1–5

quick shut the door shut the door shut the door
i want my two girls back wash it out quick
shut the door my nipples aching from grief
blood covers blood covers heat covers funk
covers semen on roses perfume skin
bone cracks lot's lies blind eyes teeth reaching
so many men so many reaching my
babies my lot's smile *please i have here two*
girls who have not known men reaching for my
babies will come from this i know i know
blood covers blood covers heat covers funk
do not wicked unto these men why ask
god's forgiveness threw my girls in the fire

The Wife of Lot After the Fire

We shall certainly deliver Lut and his followers, except for his wife; she
shall be of those who remain behind.

HOLY QUR'AN 29:32

But his wife looked back from behind him, and she became a pillar
of salt.

GEN. 19:26

He didn't warn me of what the angels told him—
I couldn't leave behind what he had done.
Someone's to blame for making me look back.
Someone ruined my mind before I could escape.

Why couldn't I leave behind what he had done?
I covered my head to keep from being ashamed.
I tell you, he ruined my mind before I could escape him,
the way he offered up our daughters to Sodom's crowd.

I covered my head to keep from being ashamed,
to keep from knowing how he brought the fire on us all.
He opened the door to give our girls to a crowd.
Why would he want to share them with those men?

I know what brought the fire on our heads,
must have lost my mind to think angels would heed me.
What kind of father tries to give his girls to a crowd of men?
What kind of God saves that man from what he deserves?

I must have lost my mind to think those angels would heed me.
They only saved my girls to bear their father's sons.
What kind of God saves a man like that from fire?
What kind of God condemns girls to carry their father's blood?

The angels only saved my girls to bear their father's sons.
No forgiveness, nothing in the hovering sky.
What kind of God condemns girls to carry their father's blood?
No mercy for me when I found out the truth.

No forgiveness in God's hovering sky,
and someone's to blame for making me look back.
If there was a chance for me and so much mercy above,
why wasn't I warned of the salt clinging to my skin?

The Two Daughters of Lot After the Fire

> And the firstborn said unto the younger, Our father is old, and there is
> not a man to come in unto us after the manner of all the earth. Come
> let us make our father drink wine, and we will lie with him that we may
> preserve the seed of our father . . .
>
> GEN. 19: 31-32

Let us remake our father
Let us show him he is small
and weak and therefore lovely
Let us pour the streams of God in his throat

Let us force this strong man who
bricked two children into the womb
Loved them above his wife
Let us force him to give us names

We do not keep with worldly
things but we learned how
He taught us to speak in psalms of wine
Go on in there now and lie with him

Let us bear this fruit on our backs
Let us die so he may live
Don't we know how
Go on in there now and lie with him

No it's all right to lie down with him
and bear his Moab and bear his Benammi
and bear his curse knocking on
our door way before that fire came

Sister
Is this a sin to remember his blood
Is this a sin to break our bodies into salt
prayers scattered at his feet

Sarah Gives Birth to Isaac

And the Lord said unto Abraham, Wherefore did Sarah laugh,
saying, Shall I of a surety bear a child, when I am old?

GEN. 18:13

Why call him Isaac
Why call him Isaac
Hagar   Hagar
Sister now I know

O my body is made again
by a God who kills with fire
O my mind has warmed
itself to the colors of sin

Why am I happy with a
man child soon to die
Why do I smile at one
who will call me *woman*

His name means laughter
His name means laughter
I am crowing out loud
I am showing my blue gums

Sarah Confronts Abraham over Hagar

Will you taste wine with me,
spit the dregs into Hagar's mouth,
dirty your fingers with her and then
stick them in my drinking bowl?

Will you take her in your bed
when my nighttime falls?
Will you breathe my perfume
then swallow her stink?

Remember we stood up
before angels together.
Man, you need to choose who will
scatter your thousand seeds.

Will you take my dry riches
then turn your back?
The girl mocks me.
I am despised in her eyes.

You better close up a well
you dug in the middle of sand.

Hagar in the Wilderness

She sent us to the wilderness
like Ham stamped with sin
Sent me and my baby to hell
like Ham stamped with sin
Raised my face to this white sky
and breathed Sarah's trouble in

Tell me what kind of woman
throws a sister out in the cold
I'm asking what kind of woman
throws a sister out in the cold
That's got to be a woman
with a desert in her soul

Fell on my knees and prayed
I asked for mercy in the sand
You know I fell down on my knees
and asked for mercy in the sand
Lifted my eyes and there stood God
a cup of water in Her hand

III

The Book of Alabama: Chapter Coltrane

for Michael S. Harper

I've been plagued by spirits   visitations
of death   fire feeding off sheeted
breath   Sometimes I see the bones
of God's back turned to me

(Hands stroke the lynch knot
and bear the cup I beg to pass
      There is no good news   I was born
as wood   a thrown match cutting
open the five wounds   On this ground
I am a minor prophet)

And sometimes I see the loins of God giving
birth to Her son   Surely there is
prayer in my horn's throat   wine
in redemption   I stand on limbo's
chasm   play   Each note shouts gospel

(Things ain't always gone be
this way   This is how to get over
      Follow the hoot owl witness
There might be consolation on the trail
grace at the tree's root   I'm bound for the other
side of water   My feet ain't meant to dangle)

Lord   I know I've been changed
The only sound is morning   I call You
by the thousand names You have
whispered to me in song
      Speak Your red clay promise
that blood cries out   rises from ash
that You will not rest on the seventh day

Five Note Range of Sorrow

for Alvin Ailey's Revelations

Wade in this spirit, work, water, code,
the five note range of sorrow that
all the church can sing. Black belt need
to shout rage with open palms,
teeth suck of cotton seed and snake
beat stick. River deep and long and sound
of ripped flesh lapping at the shore.
Scent of prayer woman drying her feet
on grass plaits Easter branches through her hair.
Scent of prayer woman spits *duende*
at the sun, her voice catching and the song ends.
The song begins and O this good news.
My Savior's blood is the Word is my people's
face turned up to blues and yes I hear
grief splinter (Jubilee and I cannot find you
Lynching tree and I cannot save you
Concrete streets and I cannot bear
to speak the names aloud again) then I see
a host dressed in billowing hope,
Holy Ghost singing loud, crowding out
the call of death in this red dirt grave.
Wade in these cries stretched forth
to mercy, runalong to evening then on to day.
Drink up the joy splashed in cupped hands:
my Lord my God and O this good news.

Day Clean

for Natasha

One ancient note
birds   their waiting throats
erupting in thanks carried
flung into the morning

My eye blessed with a *Come by here*
Held breath tangling round trees
stroking brittle raiment
the shivering awkward bones

Song splinters   *You can run*
for a long time   mouth harp through
my blood   *but Great God Almighty*
can cut you down   River can't wait

pumping testimony
I could run for a long time
but here I am this morning
born on my knees

Everyday   *Yesterday Lord*
Everyday   *Today Lord*
Everyday   *I wandered a path*
Everyday   *I tried holding on*

Fix me   *And here I am*
Fix me   *I got to speak an awful tune*
Fix me   *I got to run through grass*
Fix me   *I got to praise the muddy roots*

Prayer dappled ground   *My blues*
justified above me   Far sacred
ceiling   *Telling the story I*
traveled   Blended whimsy

Outlandish Blues (The Movie)

> . . . newly arrived Africans were classified in the North American lexi-
> con as "outlandish" in that they were "strangers to the English lan-
> guage" and had yet to learn their new roles.
>
> MICHAEL A. GOMEZ

Where else can you sail across a blue sea
into a horizon emptied of witnesses?
This is the cathartic's truth, the movie mind's eye,
a vibrant ship voyage where the slaves luckily escape,

where the horizon empties of witnesses,
and the food and the water and the mercy run low
on this photogenic voyage where slaves luckily will escape,
but not before sailors throw a few souls in the ocean.

Before the food, water and mercy run low,
watch the celluloid flashes of sexy, tight bodies
that the sailors throw into the mouths of waiting fish,
bodies branded with the Cross, baptized with holy water,

tight-packed bodies flashing across the screen,
Hollywood flat stomachs pressed to buttocks pressed to shoulders
first branded with the Cross, baptized with holy water
and then covered with manufactured filth.

The stomachs press to buttocks press to shoulders
and of course, there is no pleasure in the touch—
under the filth we can see the taut black beauty
and we guiltily consider the following:

Are we sure there was no pleasure in those touches?
Are we sure most kidnapped Africans were not full grown?
We guiltily consider the following:
Were these really children picked for long lives of work?

Are we sure these were not full grown Africans
instead of children stolen or sold from their parents,
picked for long lives of work to be squeezed from them?
Must we think on coins passed between white and black hands?

These were children stolen or sold from their parents
though we don't see any of that on the movie screen.
We don't see coins passed between white and black hands.
We don't see any boys and girls raped by the sailors.

We don't see much of their lives on the screen,
only the clean Bible one of the male slaves is given.
We don't see any boys and girls raped by the sailors,
only prayers for redemption the slave definitely receives.

There are close-ups of the Bible given to a slave
but no questions about the God he sees in his dreams.
Who gives him the redemption I'm sure he receives?
Who will he call on—the God of his parents?

Who is the God he sees in his dreams?
Who placed him in the gut of this three-hour nightmare?
Who will he call on—the God of his parents
or his Bible's Savior, a man who walks on water?

Who placed him in the gut of this three-hour nightmare?
Certainly not the God of cathartic truth
or even the Bible's Savior, a man walking across water,
just right on over blues cast like bait upon the sea.

Now with the Morning

for James Baldwin and Billy Jack Gaither

Last evening they were happy with my
black skin stripped from twigs
Their voices found my death in the night
Now with the morning their pale
knuckles must speak in tongues on their brother's skin
The rage of the song plays backwards
    The rage plays on
Lost Hebrew translated into wounds

God gave Noah the rainbow sign
Let the sins of the father be
buried for three days   *No more*
water   the fire next time   Let evil fall
to dust   blow away in a storm

They have come abandoning
my empty ashes   bringing the blood
back home to the altar   Now the whipcrack
of sheets twirls into a noose   Their brothers
crawl on broken knees to Jordan   fleeing their
keepers   The Word behind them
stamped into cooked offerings

Incident at Cross Plains
(The Lynching of William Luke, 1870)

According to my prophet's name I should
carry good news, but I only can say
God knows I am innocent. Wife, I am.
Clearly, He made us all the same and by

the rope's Word so shall we be—praying hard
then swinging but sure in this, our mission.
Now we are brothers headed for the ground.
Shall we teach Angels to cipher and read?

I want to be ready for this pine box,
ready for the Herod's days upon us.
Look for hoards of white sheets and sharpened teeth.
Fall on your knees, ask our God for mercy.

Please ask for guns, bullets, too. Love to you
and our six small ones. Wife, I die tonight.

Unidentified Female Student, Former Slave
(Talladega College, circa 1885)

You might have heard a story like this one well
but I'm telling this one to you now.
I was five when the soldiers came.

Master worked me twenty years longer.
How could I know? One day he left me alone
and an unwatched pot started to boil. By the time

he came back home I was cleaned of him and singing,
There's a man going round taking names.
Ready, set, and I was gone, walking. Could I see

beyond his yard? Did I have a thought to read or write
or count past God's creation? A barefooted
girl!—and you remember, you woman who will take

your pen to write my life. This is what the truth was like:
Master's clouds followed me to the steps of this school.
Dear reader, when you think on this years after I have died

and I am dust, think on a great and awful morning
when I learned my freedom. Think that the skin on my
back was scared when I dared step out into the world,

when my Master stood trembling and weeping
on his front porch and he cursed me beyond knowing.

Confederate Pride Day at Bama
(Tuscaloosa, 1994)

The first time, my liberal white friends try
to prepare me. I might feel ashamed when I hear
rebel yells, see the too familiar flag waving.
You know they're going to sing the song, don't you?

The fraternity boys dressed in gray uniforms,
marching boldly around the yard, then coming home to black
maids, their heads tied up in bright handkerchiefs.

Faces greased to perfection once a year. *Can you believe*
they make those women dress up like mammies?
Southern meals prepared with eye-rolling care.
You should stage a protest. For me or for my mama?

Come day, go day, God sends Sunday and I see those
sisters at the grocery store buying food every week.
We smile and sometimes meet each other's gaze.

Nod.
At the very least, write a letter. Some kinds of anger
need screaming. Some kinds just worry the gut
like a meal of unwashed greens, peas picked

too early from the field. Or a dark woman, her brow
wrapped in red, smiling to herself, then hawking
and spitting her seasoning into a Dixie cooking pot.

Aretha at Fame Studios

I could speak on a hotter than fire riot
time and a woman tying up her Detroit
promises in a rag. The prodigal child
arriving in Muscle Shoals, Alabama—hopefully
to sing freedom if only for one day.
The migration head swallowing its tail in the year of my birth.
I'm telling the truth when I say she'll meet Dr. King soon.
He'll kiss her on the cheek, tell her (damn
straight) she should demand what's due her.
And you could eat a tune served up more
than a few times, ripe pot liquor
settled around the old meat of the matter.
And I could forget the deal: she's here for business,
not to march. See the white musicians in the studio with her,
not a brother's guitar anywhere in sight?
Young boys playing so good like they've been chased
through the swamps for decades. Like they know
talk going on underneath a sister's clothes.
They got the nerve to have their eyes wide open.
She lifts her voice, starts telling tales out of school.
You're a no good heartbreaker
You're a liar and you're a cheat
Is there any doubt about the color
of the man she conjures? I could discuss her signature
key now but I'm afraid she has raised him
from the dust, he's standing on the other
side of glass and that next note, that next note
might cause him to break fool in front of white folks.
You're a no good heartbreaker
Somebody stop that man.
Somebody stop that man.
Somebody stop that sister from hollering
the naming his sins out loud blues.

Somebody close these white folks' eyes.
Somebody lie to her and keep her from crying.
Somebody tell her a little bit of sweetness
is coming her way quick.

NOTES

"The Battered Blues (1. Jones for my Blues)": *I've been downhearted ever since the day we met* combines two lines from "How Blue Can You Get," a blues song written by Jane Feather and recorded by B. B. King.

"Don't Know What Love Is": *I'm an evil gal / don't you bother with me,* are lines from "Evil Gal Blues," written by Leonard Feather and Lionel Hampton and recorded by Dinah Washington.

"Sarai Gives Hagar the Egyptian to Abram": Sarai's and Abram's names were changed to "Sarah" and "Abraham" shortly before the destruction of Sodom. Abraham is the uncle of Lot, and Hagar's son, Ishmael, is the ancestor of Zipporah, Moses' wife.

"The Wife of Lot Has a Premonition of Her Death": *Soon one morning / Death come creeping in my room . . .* are lines from a traditional spiritual.

"Day Clean": *You can run / for a long time . . . but Great God Almighty / can cut you down* are lines from a traditional spiritual.

"Outlandish Blues" contains a quote from Michael A. Gomez, *Exchanging Our Country Marks: The Transformation of African Identities in the Colonial and Antebellum South* (Chapel Hill: the University of North Carolina Press, 1998). The quote references a passage from George W. Mullin's *Flight and Rebellion: Slave Resistance in Eighteenth Century Virginia* (New York: Oxford University Press, 1972).

"Now with the Morning": On February 19, 1999, in Sylacauga, Alabama, Billy Jack Gaither, a gay white man, was beaten to death by two other white men who took turns with an ax handle; then his attackers set his body on fire.
    God gave Noah the rainbow sign / No more / water   the fire next time are lines from a traditional spiritual.

"Incident at Cross Plains (The Lynching of William Luke, 1870)": Luke, a white

Northerner, had traveled South to work at Talladega College, an Alabama school founded in 1867 to educate freed slaves. He and his black posse were seized and lynched together by a white mob who found Luke guilty of selling weapons to the black townspeople to protect themselves from the white nightriders. The mob found the black posse guilty of protecting Luke. He was given permission to pray and write a letter to his wife before he was hanged.

"Unidentified Female Student, Former Slave (Talladega College, circa 1885)": College archival records indicate that this young woman worked for her tuition, room, and board for two years. There are no records of her after 1887.

"Aretha at Fame Studios": The lines, *You're a no good heartbreaker / You're a liar and you're a cheat,* are from "I Never Loved a Man," written by Ronny Shannon and recorded by Aretha Franklin.

Fame studios is home of "Muscle Shoals Soul," the distinctive Rhythm and Blues sound associated with Atlantic Records. Many recording artists, including Little Richard and Junior Walker and the All Stars, traveled to Alabama to record with the white studio musicians of Fame, despite the fact that Little Richard insisted "R and B means real black."

ABOUT THE AUTHOR

Honorée Fanonne Jeffers has won awards from the Rona Jaffe Foundation, the Barbara Deming Memorial Fund for Women, and the Cleveland Center for Contemporary Art. She has also won the Julia Peterkin Award for Poetry. Her first book, *The Gospel of Barbecue,* was chosen by Lucille Clifton as winner of the Stan and Tom Wick Prize for Poetry. She teaches at the University of Oklahoma.

LIBRARY OF CONGRESS CATALOGING-IN-PUBLICATION DATA

Jeffers, Honorée Fanonne, 1967–
Outlandish blues / Honorée Fanonne Jeffers.
    p.   cm. — (Wesleyan poetry)
ISBN 0–8195–6583–0 (alk. paper) — ISBN 0–8195–6584–9
(pbk. : alk. paper)
1. African Americans—Poetry. I. Title. II. Series.
PS3560.E365O98 2003
811'.6—dc21   2002154353

CPSIA information can be obtained
at www.ICGtesting.com
Printed in the USA
BVHW04s0446110618
518563BV00001B/4/P

9 780819 565846